Table of Contents

The Leonardo DiCaprio Foundation (LDF)

After becoming famous as an actor, Leonardo DiCaprio (Leo) started his foundation in 1998. He was just 24. LDF works on behalf of climate change, wildlife, and threatened ecosystems.

What Does LDF Do?

Nonprofit organizations ask LDF for money. LDF decides which projects are given funds.

Leo thinks about the environment constantly. A third of the world's wildlands have disappeared since 1970. Populations of vertebrate land animals have declined by an average of 60 percent. As much as one-third of our coral reefs have died.

In the Rainforests

LDF works with Amazon tribes to protect their rights, lands, and culture. Deforestation puts their way of life at risk.

Each year, millions of acres of rainforest are deforested to plant crops, harvest wood, and drill for oil. This destroys the habitat of millions of plant and animal species.

Leo uses social media to talk about LDF and **conservation** issues. He doesn't really use it to talk about his movie projects. He has more than 50 million followers.

Childhood Matters

Leo often mentions a painting from his childhood bedroom. It showed the consequences of abusing Earth. It affected him deeply.

conservation (kahn-sur-VAY-shuhn): the protection of natural resources, animals, and plants

LDF Projects

LDF awarded 20 million dollars in 2017. Some money went to fight climate change. Some was for wildlife and wildlands. Marine life and oceans received funding. Some groups that represent **indigenous** peoples did too.

indigenous (in-DI-juh-nuhs): native to a particular place or region

LDF supported the Standing Rock Sioux Tribe in protesting oil pipelines on their land.

An LDF wildlife project helps protect elephants in 30 countries. LDF works with other organizations to do this. Fewer elephants are killed because of their work. The demand for ivory from elephant tusks has gone down.

Leo's work frequently brings him into contact with experts in conservation. Here Leo meets with Dr. Piers Sellers, an Earth scientist and former astronaut.

LDF has programs to protect **endangered** coral reefs. It also supports coral growth. One goal is to help the reefs adapt to challenging climate changes.

endangered (en-DAYN-jurd): in danger of becoming extinct

Small Things Can Be Important

Coral reefs make up less than two percent of the ocean. But one-fourth of ocean species need coral reefs to survive.

LDF supports a goal of 100 percent renewable energy. LDF **grants** are bringing solar power to rural villages in Fiji. Some places had no electricity. Others used diesel generators, which are big polluters.

grants (grants): gifts of money given by an organization for specific purposes (such as research or helping people do something)

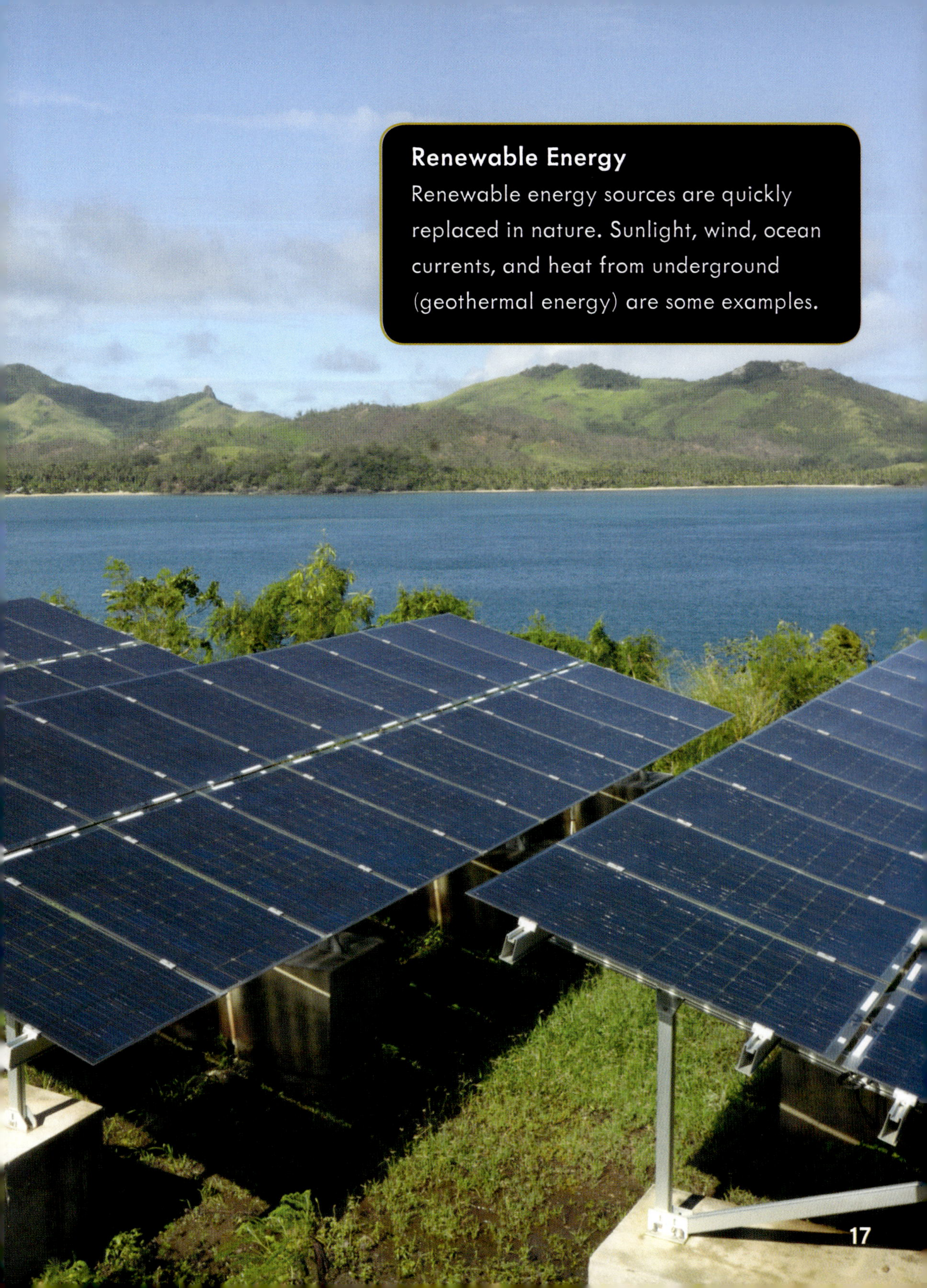

Renewable Energy

Renewable energy sources are quickly replaced in nature. Sunlight, wind, ocean currents, and heat from underground (geothermal energy) are some examples.

Leo's foundation supports indigenous rights. In the United States, it supports water education at an all-girls Lakota school. Girls study the politics, science, and history of water rights. They are encouraged to become **activists**.

activists (AK-ti-vists): people who work to help make changes in society or politics, often using strong actions, such as public protests

LDF keeps growing. Its first big grant was a million dollars for tiger conservation in Nepal in 2010. Leo's 2017 fundraiser raised 30 million dollars. Many celebrities came. Within 10 years, LDF's grants worldwide were more than 80 million dollars.

Working Together for Success

LDF and partners including the World Wildlife Fund (WWF) are aiming for 6,400 wild tigers by 2022—double the 2010 number.

Many organizations, including the Clinton Global Initiative, have honored Leo for his conservation work.

Different Organizations, Same Goals

Leo helps numerous environmental organizations. The World Wildlife Fund (WWF) is one. With help from LDF, WWF helped protect forests in Sumatra, home to endangered tigers, elephants, and orangutans.

Leo has been given a role by the United Nations (UN). He is a UN Messenger of Peace. He raises awareness of climate change.

Leo worked hard to bring about the Paris Agreement for climate change. He spoke at the signing ceremony. Later, he criticized President Donald Trump for announcing that the United States would withdraw from the agreement.

Worldwide Goals for Battling Climate Change

The Paris Agreement seeks to limit temperature increases to less than two degrees Celsius (3.6 degrees Fahrenheit). It's a challenging goal.

Leo and National Geographic made a **documentary**. It's called *Before the Flood*. The film shows climate change around the world. Leo talked to scientists. He explored how to "build a better future for our planet."

documentary (dahk-yuh-MEN-tuh-ree): a movie or television program about real situations and people

Leonardo DiCaprio at the premiere of Before the Flood

A new water beetle was discovered on Borneo in Southeast Asia. The team that found it voted to name it after Leo. They did it to honor his conservation work.

Borneo

Borneo has dense rainforests and mountains. It's the third-largest island on Earth. It lies in the southwestern Pacific Ocean.

Memory Game

Look at the pictures. What do you remember reading on the pages where each image appeared?

Index

After Reading Questions

1. Does reading about influential celebrities change or shape you view of the world and others? Explain
2. How do celebrities influence and inspire change?
3. How did the book change your belief about something?
4. How does Leonardo DiCaprio show good citizenship and contribute to the lives of people around the world?
5. What makes Leo creative, inventive, and notable?

Activity

Grantmakers are faced with difficult choices. They may want to give to many causes, but don't have enough money to go around. Find a partner. Each of you should research a different program that LDF supports. Then, prepare an argument about why your program should receive grant money. Present your arguments to a third person. Ask this person to decide which program should receive the funds and to explain why.

About the Author

Mary Hertz Scarbrough will never forget the time she got to help feed and bathe some elephants at a wildlife refuge. She also saw how many volunteers it took to prepare snacks for the animals. It was a heartwarming reminder that we can all help make the world a better place. She writes, bikes, and volunteers whenever she can from her home in South Dakota.

www.rourkeeducationalmedia.com

PHOTO CREDITS: Cover: ©Chris Pizzello/Invision/AP; page 5, 30: ©Lumeimages.com; page 7: ©luoman; page 7b: ©Sisoje; pages 8-9: ©JoyceMarrero; page 8b: ©SasinParaksa; pages 11, 30: ©Hakim atar / Shutterstock; pages 12-13, 30: ©WLDavies; page 13b: ©NASA; pages 15, 30: ©johandersonphoto; page 17: ©Rafael Ben-Ari; page 16: ©fstop123; pages 20-21, 30: ©ankitsiroya; page 21(b): ©Andrea Raffin / Shutterstocck; pages 22-23: ©Freder; page 25(a): ©a Katz / Shutterstock; pages 26-27: ©SeppFriedhuber; page 27(b): ©Kathy Hutchins / Shutterstock; page 29, 30: ©Pail Piebinga; page 29(b): ©Peter Hermes Furian

Edited by: Kim Thompson
Cover and interior design by: Rhea Magaro-Wallace

Library of Congress PCN Data

Leonardo DiCaprio / Mary Hertz Scarbrough
(Celebrity Influencers)
ISBN 978-1-73161-731-6 (hard cover)
ISBN 978-1-73161-267-0 (soft cover)
ISBN 978-1-73161-743-9 (e-Book)
ISBN 978-1-73161-755-2 (ePub)
Library of Congress Control Number: 2019932359

Rourke Educational Media
Printed in the United States of America,
North Mankato, Minnesota